MIND REHAB

MIND REHAB

The Process of Repairing What's Broken Inside and Stop Living Life by Trial and Error

---

JAMEEN R. WILLIS

Henderson, Nevada

ISBN 979-8-9950999-0-1 (print)
ISBN 979-8-9950999-1-8 (e-book))

Cover Design: Majid Kahn, fiverr.com/majid_khan786?source=inbox

Willis House Publishing
Henderson, Nevada
www.jameenwillis.com

To my wife, Nicci, and my children, Josh,
Nea, and Jonathan,
Thank you for the sacrifices you made
while I was rediscovering myself and my
purpose. I love you!

Contents

Part 4: The Improvement Phase

Part 5: The Maintaining Phase

Introduction

It was the fall of 2009—a day I will never forget. At the time, I was working from home as a Realtor. My mornings were simple: get the kids off to school, drink my coffee, get dressed, and get to work—usually with the TV on in the background, listening to the news or one of my favorite preachers on TBN. That morning, I was watching Creflo Dollar. I can't remember his exact message, but I'll never forget its impact. It had something to do with accepting what is and moving on. I don't think it was as much about the sermon itself as it was about what was going on in my life at that particular time. I remember it as vividly as if it were yesterday: I lay back on my couch, stared at the ceiling, and cried like a baby.

You see, just a day earlier, I had been notified by the IRS that they were going to place a lien on my house and every other property I owned until my back taxes were paid off. This was particularly devastating because it would completely derail my new plan to start investing in real estate.

The economy and the real estate market were at their worst. I couldn't trip and fall over a sale if I tried. Because of layoffs, many people couldn't get mortgages; companies were closing down, and lending underwriting had changed. My line of credit—the one I used as a cushion during slow months—had long since been tapped out.

I was so stressed out and didn't know what to do. I had been a Realtor for nine years and enjoyed a lucrative career in the middle of the technology boom. It was all I had done since graduating from high school and getting my real estate license.

No college degree. No Plan B to fall back on. This was the profession to which I had given my all—my time, my talents, my life! I dressed like a Realtor, drove a "Realtor car," and talked like a… well, you get the picture.

I had no rich relative to help me out until I figured things out. Well… actually, I did have relatives who inspired me. When I was a kid, my aunt and uncle influenced me to become a Realtor. They owned a real estate company in my hometown of Cincinnati, Ohio. They used to pick me up in their Cadillac to spend weekends with my cousins.

Seeing a successful Black-owned business in the eighties was rare and a major source of inspiration for me. Some people dream of being a doctor, a lawyer, or a pro athlete. But me? I had always wanted to be a "businessman."

When the 2008 recession hit, it hit my family and many other small businesses the hardest. I saw my inspiration and my heroes fall. What was once inspiration now looked like desperation. If the people I looked up to were struggling, then what the hell was I supposed to do?

To make things even more complicated, I had just gotten married a year prior. We were a blended family—my son was six, and my stepdaughter was five.

So, let's stop and recap the situation: newly married, two kids, self-employed, in the worst economy the U.S. had seen in decades. And my profession was among the hardest hit. One of the worst feelings as a husband and a father is not being able to provide for your family. I loved being a provider and doing things for my wife and kids. It felt like my ability to provide had been taken away. How was I going to sell houses to people if nobody could buy?

Being a Realtor was a huge part of my identity, and now it felt like that part of me had been stripped away. So, who was I now?

So many emotions were swirling at that time: stress, worry, and the feeling of failure. It's one thing to struggle by yourself, but it's another thing when you are struggling and have a wife and kids depending on you. Financial problems are one of the biggest causes of marital issues, and we had plenty of them.

In the real estate industry, there are different paths: sales, development, and investing in rental property or rehabbing houses. After a few years as a Realtor, I knew I wanted to invest in rehabs and rental properties.

I bought my first property in 2002: a multi-family building with a vacant bar attached. I rehabbed the bar and turned it into an apartment for myself. During this process, I fell in love with renovation. Taking a "dump" house, rehabbing it, and making it look like something meant everything to me. I enjoyed this way more than being a Realtor. It allowed me to be creative, artistic, and hands-on. I developed a passion for improving things and making them better than they were before.

And that's why the whole situation was so depressing. Just as I was planning on taking a step up to rehabbing, I was knocked several steps back. I felt lost and defeated. Instead of being in a place where I could rehab houses that most people considered "dumps," I was in the dumps myself.

Then I realized I needed to make a shift. Instead of rehabbing houses, I needed to rehab my mind! I found some "cracks" in my foundation that needed to be repaired. Just like a house has components that become old, outdated, and no longer work, what I'd been doing and how I'd been doing it weren't working anymore. I needed to work on myself.

And that's exactly what I did. Using the renovation process as a model, I developed a way to rehab my mind—one that helped me discover who I am and who I'm not.

It probably saved my life. It most definitely changed it. My intention in sharing this with you is simple: I want you to be able to rehab your mind, too. This process is already changing how I—and many others—think, make decisions, and understand our purpose. It is allowing others to discover their passions and what they are gifted at.

Who knew that while I had plans to rehab houses, I would discover and develop a plan to help rehab minds?

So here it is—***Mind Rehab***—the process of taking negative, self-defeating thoughts, actions, and emotions, and replacing them with positive, true ones.

It's rehab time!

PHASE ONE: PLANNING

Chapter 1

Self-Assessment Inspection

One of the first steps when rehabbing a house—after selecting the property—is to conduct a thorough inspection. During this process, we determine what's old, outdated, and no longer serves the house. When the inspection is complete, we have an itemized list of both mandatory and recommended repairs needed before making improvements and moving in.

We must do the same thing when rehabbing our minds. Before you can rebuild anything, you must pause long enough to take inventory. You look at the thoughts you've been living with, the beliefs you've carried for years, and the patterns that keep showing up. This personal inspection isn't about judgment—it's about honesty.

For some, conducting this assessment of current conditions may feel like a "tune-up" or a "paint and carpet" type of rehab—just a few small adjustments. But once you get into it, you may discover it requires a complete overhaul! For others, you may feel like a total wreck, willing to try anything because you don't know what to do anymore. Pump the brakes. You might not be the "ugly house" you think you are.

I've observed that people are generally good, but life deals them some bumps and bruises along the way. In real estate, we call a house worth rehabbing one with "good bones," meaning the framework and foundation are still sound. Well, *you* have "good bones" too. Your life is valuable. You have infinite potential, and the time you invest in improving yourself is well worth it.

So, let's get to it.

Chapter 2

What's Not Working Anymore?

It's inspection time—your inspection. Time to get real. Time to be honest with yourself about where you really are in life. What's not working anymore? When inspecting a house, we check the furnace, the water heater, the central air, the plumbing, the electrical, the roof, and the gutters—all the systems that keep the home functioning. Some things are just old and outdated. Other things were improperly installed or never should have been there in the first place.

In my 25 years in real estate, I have seen a little bit of everything, from pea-green or mustard-colored refrigerators to "Little House on the Prairie" wallpaper and electrical panels that look like a 4-year-old's latest art project. That pea-green refrigerator may have been poppin' in 1956, but now? Not so much.

When you plan to rehab a house, you have to check and document what's not working; otherwise, you risk overlooking something that could keep the house from selling or renting. Some people try to save money by not replacing things that really need to go.

As we begin rehabbing our minds, we must do the same.

When I first began this process in 2009, it had become glaringly clear that I needed to consider doing something else. Relying on real estate commissions as my main source of income was no longer working. As I mentioned earlier, the economy and housing market were in terrible shape, and I was struggling financially.

I was 19 when I earned my real estate license in Ohio. Not bad for a kid from a broken home—a kid most considered a statistic or an "at-risk" teen. I grinded, hustled, and built my business. At 22, when most of my friends and classmates were graduating from college, I had already bought my first house, had a nice car, and had been established in my career for years.

Being self-employed was very cool; it was what I'd always wanted. Even as a kid, I used to draw boardrooms with a lawyer, accountant, marketing person, and me as the CEO. It felt good not to have a boss standing over my shoulder, telling me what to do.

Between 2003 and 2006, I experienced several major life events. I had a son and broke up with his mother after a long-term relationship. I lost my mother to pancreatic cancer in 2005. All these changes, combined with the downsides of being self-employed, left me living with my grandparents again. I had lost momentum. I left the company my family owned and joined RE/MAX to move forward in the industry.

By 2007, I'd gotten my grind back and was rebuilding. I met my wife, Nicci. I got my credit back in order and bought a four-bedroom house just a couple of streets over from my grandparents'. After that, I found a good deal on the Mercedes I wanted and drove with my cousin to Indiana to pick it up.

I even started my first investment company, Custom Contemporary Properties. I had always planned to transition from real estate sales to investing in rentals and rehab projects. Nicci, my soon-to-be fiancée, helped me get started and went in with me on the first property.

It seemed to be all coming together. I would keep selling houses to pay the bills while building my other business by acquiring rentals and flipping properties.

And then, the market crashed.

Everything I'd worked so hard for dried up. I had pushed myself in a career that wasn't a natural fit just to get to the next step—and then the bottom fell out.

At the same time, something else wasn't working for me: the version of Christianity I'd been taught all my life. I'd started teaching a Wednesday night Bible study at my church, which really got me digging into the Word. I discovered so many things that I didn't know or understand before.

As I delved deeper into the study of religion and God, I felt bamboozled, like the wool had been pulled over my eyes. I realized how much of what I'd been taught had been built on artificial rules used to control and coerce people into obedience.

I've always had an interest in God and spirituality. I was baptized when I was 12, but I got serious about Christianity around age 20. Church became a priority; I believed in it and depended on it with all my heart. Not only did I consider myself "saved," but I felt—and still feel—that being a Christian and going to church saved my life. It gave me hope and something to trust when I needed it most. I have been through a lot, and I know I couldn't have made it without my relationship with God.

However, I went on a spiritual journey to discover "truth" and what it really meant to have a relationship with Christ. There were just so many things about religion that, after much study, I didn't agree with anymore. They weren't effective in my life.

And honestly, I felt let down by God, too. If you've ever felt that way, you're not alone. We'll talk more about that later, but for now, just know this: feeling disappointed doesn't disqualify your faith. It just means you're human.

So now it's your turn.

Think about your life and what you are doing. Think about where you are spending the most time and energy. Identify what's not working anymore. What do you possibly need to cut out or change?

For me, it was being a full-time Realtor and religion. For you, it might be a relationship, a habit, a mindset, or a job. It might be the pattern of putting yourself on the back burner.

This is the time to identify what you have been doing that

has been yielding undesired results. Just because you have been doing something for a long time doesn't necessarily mean you are doing it at the *right* time.

Chapter 3

What Has Never Worked?

By this point, you may be thinking, "Oh, shit, my life is a mess." But don't worry; help is on the way.

In the last chapter, we talked about what isn't working anymore. In this part of the inspection, we focus on what has *never* worked.

When I look at potential properties, one of the main things I search for are features that were never a good idea in the first place, or that won't work for today's homeowner. It might be a full bathroom right off the kitchen, or a house in the Arizona desert with no central air. Some things were just never a good idea. But for lack of resources or a better plan, people endured dysfunctional dwellings for years. They adjusted. They tolerated. They made it work… even though it never really worked.

For me, being a Realtor wasn't working, but I had to ask: why? Things happen to people all the time—family problems, financial problems, health problems. But challenges don't necessarily mean you are doing the wrong thing.

I had to look closely at *why* being a Realtor wasn't working for me. What's the main thing a Realtor is supposed to do? Sell! It's sales, people! And that is almost the exact opposite of what I am naturally wired to do.

You see, even though I have been a Realtor for over 25 years and have sold hundreds of houses, sales isn't my gift. I'm trained in it, and I worked hard to build that career, but at my core, I'm an introvert and a creative, analytical visionary! It wasn't until years of struggling to fit into a puzzle that wasn't made for me that I realized real estate sales wasn't the best profession for my natural talents.

How do you know what you are gifted at? Some people feel they have never discovered their gift. I heard comedian Steve Harvey describe it as "what you do best with the least amount of effort."

Think about how easy it is for Jay-Z to come up with a verse for a song. For others, crafting a song takes days, maybe weeks.

I once tried to assemble a dresser I bought from IKEA. It took me three days and two bottles of Corona, and I still had four parts left over! My wife, on the other hand? She put together the next item in about 45 minutes while watching Netflix at the same damn time. (I must confess: my wife is the one who puts things together in our household).

One of my favorite books, *The Big Leap* by Gay Hendricks, describes what you are not good at as the "Zone of Incompetence." Many of us spend years living in that space.

We do things that don't "work" for us for many reasons: the pay is stable, it's what our family expects, or it's the social norm.

And let me be clear: I'm not only talking about a job. We need to look at the "big picture." What has never worked for you in *all* areas of life?

Are you like me, in an industry that doesn't fit your gifts? Has being single never worked because you crave companionship, even though "not being tied down" sounded good? Were you forced into an organization you despised? Does where you live not match who you want to be?

We do things that never work because of money, fear of failure, or simply because we don't know what *does* work for us. We haven't found our "Zone of Genius."

Over time, doing things that don't work takes a mental toll. We start to think something is wrong with us. But in many instances, we are simply in the wrong positions, places, and spaces.

A fish on land looks out of place, right? Put it back in water, and it thrives. The same is true for us.

It may take some time and thought, but now is the time for self-inspection. Go ahead. Take a good, hard look and ask yourself: "What have I been doing that has never worked for me?"

Chapter 4

Examining Your Negative Thoughts, Decisions,

and Feelings Right Now

By now, you are probably more attuned to how you're feeling. I know I was. Once I identified what I wasn't good at and what wasn't working for me, I felt stuck. Sure, I knew what *wasn't* right for my life, but I had no idea how—or when—I could start doing what *was* right. Change sounds great until you remember… bills. Responsibilities. Real life.

Doing the wrong thing for a long time wears you down mentally. You begin to think you aren't good at anything. You tell yourself, "I'm a failure. Something is wrong with me. I feel like giving up. I don't know how I will ever get out of this situation."

Those were the thoughts running through my mind, and they had me feeling—for lack of a better word—like shit.

Remember the "fish out of water" example I used earlier? Have you ever felt like that fish? Completely out of place, just trying to survive? Waking up in the morning hating where you're about to go, knowing that for several hours you'll be around people who don't think like you, don't operate like you, and don't understand you?

How does that relate to houses? They say beauty is in the eye of the beholder. Seeing the potential in a house—despite how it looks, smells, and functions—is a skill that can be cultivated. You learn to look past the mess and see the masterpiece.

Sure, there may be a lot wrong with the house, but you can still see what it *could* be. And that's exactly how we have to look at ourselves.

We can have the wrong outlook on life and ourselves, just like the people who pass by a messed-up house and miss a great property or a killer deal. You're a great investment! No matter your current condition, how old you are, how "outdated" you may feel, or how broken you are, you and the rest of your life represent a great opportunity.

Now, it's self-assessment time. It's time to take inventory and inspect where you are right now. What are your negative thoughts, actions, and feelings *right now*? I want you to actually write them down. Make a list. Go ahead and get it all out. Getting it on paper helps; it's a form of release. You can't repair what you don't reveal.

We will use this list later to develop our Mind Rehab Blueprint.

Chapter 5

What Have You Never Done (or Even Tried to Do)?

Sometimes, the problem is not what's wrong or broken—it's what's missing.

We can get so caught up in trying to make what we're doing work that we don't even consider other options. Why? Because doing something else requires effort, change, and, most likely, an uncomfortable level of vulnerability. Trying something else can sometimes feel like admitting defeat. We feel like we're acknowledging failure.

As far as my career in real estate was concerned, it was all or nothing. No Plan B. I was all in on being a Realtor. I had decided this was going to work, and I was determined to force it to work—even while I was deeply frustrated that it *wasn't* working.

When I look at houses, I ask, "What's not there that *could* be there? What hasn't been added to this house that might increase its value? Can I add a bedroom or finish the basement to add value? Will removing a wall or relocating a bathroom make the house more functional?"

These same questions apply to life.

When faced with a problem or stuck in a situation, it helps to ask yourself: "What's possible? What perspective or option have I overlooked?"

Hate where you live? When was the last time you took a

vacation? Have you considered transferring your job or business to another city?

When I first started this process, I realized I had never tried anything other than being a Realtor. It was all I had done since graduating from high school. I had gone all out and given it my all, never even considering another path.

This is all part of the planning phase of your Mind Rehab. I want you to think about your life as a whole and how things have been going. But also think about what you could possibly be missing. What options are you not exploring?

Here are some thought-provoking questions:

- When was the last time you took a vacation to a new place or somewhere you have considered moving?

- When was the last time you visited another church or researched different spiritual teachings?

- Have you explored another aspect of your current professional field?

- Could you turn a hobby—something you are good at and do for free—into a profession or business?

Chapter 6

What Do You R.E.A.L.L.Y. Want?

"I have found Proverbs 29:18 to be true not only in life, but also in rehabbing houses: "*Where there is no vision, the people perish* (KJV). One of the biggest lessons I've learned is this: you must *envision* the finished product *before* you ever pick up a hammer. You need a vision—clear, detailed, and compelling—before the work begins.

When I look at a potential investment property, I visualize what it *could* be when it's all fixed up. From there, I create a plan—a "scope of work" that details everything needed to make that vision a reality.

Some people jump right into a project with no written plan, no blueprint, and no scope of work. That can be dangerous. You must count the costs of a rehab project. How much money is needed? How long will it take? What is the right order to follow for the renovation?

If that's true for a piece of real estate, it's even more critical when rehabbing our minds. We must have a clear scope of work and a blueprint for the process. Before you can create that blueprint, you need to make assessments, complete inspections, and get estimates.

The major question we need to answer is: In your life, are you doing what you **R.E.A.L.L.Y.** want? Are you living the life that you **R.E.A.L.L.Y.** want? Don't worry; we'll break down this acronym in a minute.

First, take a deep breath and ask yourself: If money weren't an issue, what would you be doing? If you could remove the fear of not fulfilling the roles, responsibilities, and obligations you currently have, what would your life look like?

Ask yourself, "What do I *really* want?" This is where your vision begins.

To help you gain clarity, I created an assessment to help you determine what you **R.E.A.L.L.Y.** want. This will become part of your Mind Rehab Blueprint—your personal scope of work to shift your thinking, rediscover your gifts, and build a life aligned with your purpose.

Self-Assessment: What Do You R.E.A.L.L.Y. Want?

R–Right:
- Is your goal, career, or business right for you?
- Do you have the gifts, talents, and abilities to do "it" well?

E–Enjoy:
- Do you enjoy what you are doing?
- Are you constantly watching the clock, waiting for the day to end, or do you wake up in the morning excited about the day ahead?

A–Always: (We become what we think about.)
- What do you think about *always*?
- What occupies your mind the most?

L–Love: (It's hard to do something day in and day out with excellence without love.)
- Do you have the passion to endure the sacrifice, discipline, and perseverance required?

L–Leave:
- Is it worth what you've had to leave behind—or what you may need to leave behind?
- Is the trade-off worth it?

Y–You: (What you R.E.A.L.L.Y. want should come from within you—not others.)
- What's motivating you?
- Is it truly *you*—or is it the expectations, opinions, and pressures of others?

"Mind Rehab" Tip: Stop buying the opinions of others; it will leave you mentally broke!

If these questions stir something in you, if they make you pause, reflect, or realize you may need a major shift, then it's time for Mind Rehab.

Hard hats on. The Vision Phase begins.

Chapter 7

The Mind Rehab Blueprint

Through my own journey, I discovered something powerful: the same process that makes a house rehab successful can transform your mind and your life. The steps, the phases, the order—it all works. And honestly, by the time you finish this book, you might even feel like you could rehab a house, too.

So, let's get right to it.

This is the Mind Rehab Blueprint. These first six chapters have walked you through the Planning Phase—the problems, the pain points, and what's "broken." By now, you should have a clearer picture of what needs your attention.

The following chapters will focus on finding the solutions. Before we dive into renewing your mind, let's review the blueprint and the order of the process. Just like every house renovation is different, every life is different. Some phases may take longer for you than for someone else, but the process itself remains the same.

- **Phase 1:** The Planning Phase

- **Phase 2:** The Demolition Phase

- **Phase 3:** The Restoration Phase

- **Phase 4:** The Improvement Phase

- **Phase 5:** The Maintaining Phase

This blueprint has carried me through some of my darkest times

and brought me into some of my brightest days. It has been effective for me and many others who have put it into practice. Since we're going through this journey together, I'm going to address you from time to time as "Rehabber."
Cool? Trust me, now is not the time to stop!

Hard hat on, Rehabber! We're just getting started.

PHASE 2: DEMOLITION

Chapter 8

Clearing Out What Holds You Back

In the planning phase, we identified our negative, self-defeating thoughts, actions, and feelings. You made your lt back in Chapter Four, and now it's time to "demo" those habits—whether they're mental, physical, or emotional.

The demolition process is a little different with Mind Rehab than it is with rehabbing houses. Let's take, for example, replacing a refrigerator that's too small for your needs. Maybe it's just plain ugly, but it still works. You don't want to throw out the old refrigerator before buying a new one.

It's the same way with rehabbing your mind. You get rid of the negative thoughts, actions, and feelings by introducing new ones. And not just any new thoughts, but positive, truthful ones. Actions and decisions that are what you R.E.A.L.L.Y want. And new feelings that come from knowing what I call the real "YOU."

New Thoughts

It's been said that we are what we think about all day long. Your thoughts are the first things to swap out in the mind-rehab process. You see, our thoughts determine our actions, and our actions determine how we feel.

The average person has between 6,000 and 70,000 thoughts per day. And of these thousands of thoughts, about ninety percent of them are repetitive. What's even more concerning is the fact that about eighty percent of the repetitive thoughts are NEGATIVE! Why is this?

Some say this is a survival mechanism that helped our ancestors avoid danger. I also believe it's because our culture has developed a "negative default." By that, I mean we automatically think negatively because it is ingrained in our current culture. We greet each other with, "How are you holding up?" We respond with, "Not too bad." We say things like, "I probably won't win, but here goes nothing."

People say it's better not to get your hopes up, so you're not disappointed when things don't work out. What a terrible way to live, right?

I not only want to help you change your thoughts from those of the average person, but I also want to help you avoid *being* the average person! Who says you have to think like and be the average person? That's a choice we make, and we can choose to change our thoughts.

A critical part of Mind Rehab is not only improving the *quality* of your thoughts but also reducing the *quantity*. You can do this through meditation, exercise, affirmations, and other practices we'll explore later.

Now let me be clear: it's simply unrealistic to expect to never have a negative thought. The point is to limit the number of your thoughts overall, reduce negative ones, and increase positive ones.

Remember when I talked about your life feeling "old" and "outdated"? Well, your thought life is a major reason you feel that way. Just like an old, worn-out carpet, your thoughts have worn you down.

It's time to introduce new thoughts—thoughts that are positive, thoughts that reflect what you want, who you are, and where you're going. Just like you can change the default settings on your computer or phone, you can change the defaults in your life. When you are on "default," your thoughts are mostly negative and average at best. If we're being honest, over ninety percent of the time, we're on default without real-izing it, unconscious and unaware.

Our thought life is so important. You can't *do* anything different unless you *know* something different. And you most certainly can't know something different unless you think something different.

Negative Choices, Actions, and Decisions

Too many negative thoughts and not enough positive, truthful ones lead to poor choices. If you think, "I'm a failure," you'll act like one. It really is that simple.
Rehabbing a house is not rocket science—neither is rehabbing your mind. But you do have to follow the process.

It's hard to move when you think, *"I'm stuck."* And even harder to take action when you *feel* stuck.

Sometimes we can have tunnel vision and see only the conditions right in front of us. One of the biggest breakthroughs in my life was developing a "bird's-eye view," the ability to zoom out and see the big picture rather than just the current situation.

When faced with making a big decision or an important choice, ask yourself, "What's possible?" We tend to err on the side of what's happened before. Negative choices become habits because they feel familiar. Without "intervention" or "rehab," the mind and body seek that familiar feel. A habit is a craving for a "familiar feeling."

Negative Feelings

When I was in kindergarten, I attended a small Catholic school with small class sizes. After the school year ended, I remember the teacher meeting with my mom. To this day, I still remember the fear that I was in trouble or that something was wrong. Instead, the teacher said they believed I was advanced and wanted to test me in higher-level classes.

The following year, for the first week, I was placed in differ-ent classes and at different grade levels to see where I would be challenged. At the end of the week, the school met again with my mother and recommended that I skip first grade and go straight to second grade.

I will never forget how that made me feel. I felt like a genius, the smartest kid in the world. My mother told the teacher that she would give it some thought. She was concerned that I, as a younger, smaller first grader, might be bullied, that, although I was intellectually advanced, I might be socially immature.

She decided that it would be best for me to stay in my "right" grade for my age and not skip the first grade. I don't remember being disappointed that I didn't get to skip a grade. Just the simple fact that they thought I was smart enough to skip the first grade was good enough for me! The feeling stayed with me. It boosted my confidence at a young age and shaped how I saw myself. It gave me the confidence to try, do, and accomplish many things I might not have tried otherwise.

I know we are talking about negative feelings right now, but I wanted to tell you that story to show you how powerful feelings are. During this process, you will see that feelings are among the most important aspects of Mind Rehab.

When you feel low, you perform low. When you have negative feelings, you behave negatively. Thoughts, actions, and feelings go hand in hand; they are inseparable. You can think your way into depression. One can imagine things not working out and feel the weight of it before it happens.

Ridding Yourself of Negative Thoughts

Thoughts become things when you feel them. This works both positively and negatively. Your subconscious can't distinguish between good and bad, or right and wrong. It only registers what *is*. And what *is*, is the sum total of your thoughts, actions, and emotions.

Removing the negative thoughts, actions, and emotions that have been holding you back requires you to introduce new ones. Mind Rehab will show you how to do just that.

When renovating a house, you assess the current condition and identify what needs to be removed. Then you develop a vision of how you want the finished product to be and develop a plan.

And that is exactly what we're going to do with our minds.

Thousands of houses that could be great new homes for someone are overlooked because their current condition keeps them from being sold.

Are you ready to get rid of the stuff that's been holding you back? Do you want to finally get unstuck with your life?

Hard hats on!

Chapter 9

Your False Self and How Not to Be Fooled by It

One of the most important skills for being a successful investor is the ability to determine the condition of the things that matter most in a house. For the average consumer, the beautiful floors, custom cabinets, tile, and fresh landscaping are the major selling points.

Not so much with investors.

We look at the roof, the foundation, the framework. We look at the things that make a house "run" —things like plumbing, electrical, heating, ventilation, and cooling. Sure, the updated finishes are a plus, but those can be swapped out more easily.

This is where many first-time flippers and homeowners make costly mistakes. They focus on paint, flooring, cabinets, and fixtures, overlooking the most important aspects of a house. If you don't follow the renovation process in the proper order, you'll end up starting over, redoing work, and wasting money.

The finishings can fool you. This is how shady flippers get over on people. They slap on some new paint and carpet on a property and call it "flipped," while avoiding the most important repairs that take the most time and money to fix.

And the truth is that we do the same thing with our minds!

Your False Self

When I got my real estate license in 1999, it felt good. I was a 19-year-old kid selling houses to people twice my age. I had what most would consider a rough childhood, and it was a blessing to become an entrepreneur and do something positive with my life.

I was proud of becoming a Realtor. It gave me an identity and a sense of purpose.

At 19, identity was everything.

In business, there is a phrase— "faking it until you make it." And that is what I did. I wore some non-prescription glasses to look a bit older. I wore a shirt and tie most days (I was used to dressing in business attire because we were required to at the vocational school I attended; I like having a good reason to dress up). I removed the gold tooth I'd gotten at 14 because I wanted to look more "professional." I even traded in my black Mazda with chrome rims for a more "conservative" and "professional-looking" Ford Contour. I was committed to the image.

Our careers, jobs, and titles can have such a strong influence on our lives that we start to identify those roles or jobs as who we are. We believe we are what we do. And this is exactly what I did. I identified with being a Realtor so much that when the real estate market crashed, and my ability to be a successful Realtor was severely affected, I had an identity crisis.

The problem with identifying who you are by what you do is that if you lose what you do, you lose who you are. That's why CEOs of companies take their lives or fall into depression when they lose their positions. That's why a person falls apart after a divorce or the death of a loved one. Your identity is so tied to being someone's spouse, mother or father, or son or daughter that you don't know how to function when they are gone.

Your False Self: The EGO

Just like so many would-be homeowners think that paint, flooring, and finishes are the most important aspects of home improvement, we all too often let what we do, have, and accomplish determine our worth. This is one of the biggest problems and hindrances to our personal development and knowing the real YOU.

The EGO. It's the false self. It's the identity crisis that's probably holding you up from living the life that you R.E.A.L.L.Y want.

Characteristics of the False Self:

I am what others think of me.

This is true whether the thoughts are good or bad. If someone says something negative to you, you believe it. If someone praises you, but stops, you lose the source of your confidence. Have you ever noticed that when someone speaks negatively about you, you become upset? That's because, to some degree, you believe what they said is true. How you feel about yourself should come from within, not from someone else.

Mind Rehab Tip: Stop "buying" the opinions of others. It will leave you mentally broke.

I am what I do.

This applies to your career and your roles at home. I told you how deeply I identified with being a Realtor. It had become so much a part of my identity that when I was no longer doing it, I didn't know what to do. I didn't know who I was.

This is particularly triggering for men. We identify heavily with what we do for a living. Losing the ability (or the *perceived* ability) to provide can weigh heavily on a man's heart and mind.

Identifying yourself by what you do can make you feel inadequate as a man or woman. If you think about it, no matter how long you have had a job or career, you once didn't, so how is that who you are? Before you were a husband or wife, father or mother, brother or sister, you were just YOU.

Mind Rehab Tip: "I do what I do because of who I am; I am not who I am because of what I do.

I am what I have.

Possessions—who doesn't like to have them? We must make sure that we have them and they don't have us. Have you ever lost a car or a house before? You may have worked hard to get those things, but that thing is not you. You are less valuable because you don't have many possessions.

You can fall into the trap of waiting to "live" until you have the "right" house, clothes, or car. Things come and go. Possessions can be lost and regained. Your possessions are not the essence of who you are.

I am my accomplishments.

Winners and losers. Awards and benchmarks. They all appeal to the senses, evoking either positive or negative feelings. What happens when the accomplishments slow down or stop altogether? Have you ever thought that you won't be happy with yourself until you accomplish… (fill in the blank)?

I am separate from others.

We all come from the same Source. The Bible even states in Romans 2:11— *"For God does not show favoritism"* (NIV). The feeling that "no one understands me" and "I am not like everyone else" is not true. The truth is, everyone is special and different, but not everyone is aware of it.

God has placed a specific expression of His love in every one of us. And if it's all from the same Source, then we must all be connected.

Things like politics, religion, and race separate us. You may have the exact expression of God's love (gift or talent) that someone wants or needs, but the sense of separation caused by the ego identity prevents this connection.

That is why I love the term *"namaste."* It means, "I honor the God in you, which also is in me." This is a great reminder that we're all connected spiritually. I believe the world would be a much better place if we became more aware and reminded ourselves that we're all connected and that no one is better than another.

I am separate from God.

This is the most damaging lie of the ego, causing you to believe you are separate from God. The ego says, "There's God in the sky, and then there's me here on earth." But the truth is that God is with us at all times, and it is impossible for you to be separated from Him.

Initially, you may have difficulty understanding and accepting this truth because of how you were raised as a child. If God is the Source of all things, then you and I came from God. And if we come from God, then we are connected to Him.

We will go over this in detail in the following chapters. But for now, know that you are not separate from God. To feel separated from God is the true definition of being unsaved, unconscious, and unaware. But Jesus tells us in Luke 17:21: *"The Kingdom of God is within."*

I think author and spirituality teacher, Wayne Dyer, says it best: "You can be a host to God, or a hostage to your ego. It's your call."

How Not to Be Fooled by It

The identity crisis of the false self can have you sitting on the sidelines for years. It can have you waiting until you do more, have more, are more to "live." The ego can make you think your best days are behind you and that they may never return.

I want you to think about each characteristic of the ego and how, if you really think about it, this can't be the real YOU.

You haven't always had whatever you have now, so that can't be you. There was a time when you didn't do what you do now, so that's not you either. And opinions? They come and go. People change their opinions, and their thoughts and opinions are out of our control anyway. So how can they define who we are?

There's a line in the movie, *The Usual Suspects,* that says, "The greatest trick the Devil ever pulled was convincing the world that he didn't exist." I have a different take on this. The greatest trick in the world is convincing you that the God in YOU doesn't exist. Don't be fooled by your false self telling you that you are separate from God.

Chapter 10

Getting Rid of the Source of Your Negative Thoughts, Actions, and Feelings

Everyone—whether you're aware of it or not—has a "driver." There is something that makes you think the way you think, do what you do, and feel how you feel.

If we are going to rehab our minds, we need to get to the source—the root—the main area of the ego we have unconsciously identified with. Usually, it's one specific thing that's got us "trippin." To fix it, we need to revisit the parts of the ego and determine which one we have falsely gravitated toward.

Mind Rehab Tip: You can't heal what you don't reveal. You can't fix what you haven't identified as broken.

I'm not trying to put words in your mouth, but here are some examples to help you identify the one area you most need to tackle:

- **"I'm a failure"**: This connects to the "
- **I am what I do"** and **"I am my accomplishments"** parts of the ego.
- **"I am all alone"**: This ties to the **"I am separate from everyone"** part of the ego.
- **"I feel hopeless"**: This connects to the **"I am separate from God"** part of the ego.

And don't feel bad; you're in good company. We've all, at different times, falsely identified with failure, loss, loneliness, and disappointment.

Feeling Let Down

Have you ever felt disappointed by God? This can be one of the hardest things to bounce back from. You prayed and asked God for help, but nothing happened as you expected. You trusted God to come through and make a way for you, only to be embarrassed and feel left on your own.

This is one of the reasons some people walk away from faith altogether. They stop believing because they feel like God didn't come through. Some even become atheists.

But the Bible helps with this feeling of separation from God when things don't go our way:

> *For I am convinced that neither death nor life, neither angels nor demons, neither the present nor the future, nor any powers, neither height nor depth, nor anything else in all creation, will be able to separate us from the love of God... — Romans 8:38-39*

Nothing can separate us from the love of God—not disappointment, not confusion, and not even prayers that seem to go unanswered.

The Source of the Wound

When I was about thirteen or fourteen, I got into an argument with my mother. When I was growing up, my mother had a drinking problem, and our relationship was "strained," to say the least. On this particular day, she was likely recovering from being intoxicated.

I don't remember what the argument was about or how it started, but it escalated to the point where I said I didn't want to live with her anymore. She responded by throwing a pot at me and yelling, "I hate you!"

I didn't just hear words; I heard a verdict: *"You are not loved."* Those words lodged in my soul. I figured if she does not love me, I must be unlovable.

I may not remember the argument, but I will *never* forget how those words made me feel. What my mother spoke that day were the most damaging words anyone has ever said to me. It wasn't until I was well into my thirties that I realized her words were the source of my struggle with self-love. Having a parent—the person who should be your primary influence—tell you they don't love you can make you feel worthless if you let it.

This is why it's so important to identify the source of our feelings and their impact on how we show up in the world.

The **"I am what others think of me"** characteristic of the ego had me tripping for a long time. Deep down, even though I didn't think about it every day, I didn't value myself the way I should have. I felt that if my own mother didn't love me, how valuable could I really be?

You may be reading this and thinking, "Of course your mom loved you." And you're right. She did. I realize now that she spoke out of anger and the influence of alcohol. But at the time, I was led by my ego.

This is my whole point: You can't "buy" the opinions of others, good or bad. Your sense of value and self-worth has to come from **YOU**. And you, and only you, have the power to determine that value.

PHASE 3: RESTORATION

Chapter 11

Fixing the "Cracks" in Your Mental Foundation

Restoration is by far the most important part of the Mind Rehab process. It's the part that allows you to focus on the top priority in your life: **YOU**. It's time to get to the real YOU.

In the following chapters, we will rediscover what you're great at and what I call "Your Genius." The Restoration Phase is when I finally felt unstuck and gained clarity on who I am as a person seeking to fulfill my purpose.

Don't Be Led By Your "Or"

Being led by the ego is like having a crack in your mental foundation. A "crack" in your mental foundation shows up as an identity crisis. It has you thinking you *are* what you *do* and *have*. I call it the "Er-Or Syndrome." You know: Doct**or**, Lawy**er**, Realt**or**, Sing**er**… as if your title is your identity. As we have already seen, it convinces you that you are what others think of you and that you are separate from God.

Just like a house needs a solid roof, foundation, and framework to be a house, you, too, have a covering, foundation, and framework that make up the real YOU.

Sometimes you don't even notice the crack until you go through the demolition process—until you strip away what you do, what you have, and what others think of you. Only then can you see what's been damaged.

Mind Rehab Tip: You can't heal what you don't reveal.

Repairing a cracked foundation is critical to maintaining a house's structural integrity. In the same way, you must fix the cracks in YOUR structure.

What is your foundation? Your foundation is made up of the core principles, morals, and beliefs that you live by. Your mental foundation is where your self-esteem and confidence come from. If your foundation is cracked, you can't add anything to it—the structure simply won't withstand the weight.

If your foundation is cracked right now, it's time to stop and take a break so that YOU don't break. Burnout is real. Crashing out is real. And we don't have time to crash out right now. You got bail money?!

The Repair Method

You repair the cracks in your mental foundation by discovering the real YOU—your gifts and your genius. Here's how the repair process works:

- **Inspect the crack:** When I first went through this process, my mental crack was the belief that I was a failure.

- **Identify the cause:** I couldn't sell houses and couldn't provide for my family, so I *felt* like a failure. That was the main issue: identifying with the *cause* rather than with the **SOURCE**.

- **Prep the area:** I had to stop and assess my career and what I was currently doing to provide. For me, the situation was my profession. Your situation may be different, but baby, a crack is a crack. Lay out the dysfunction of how you currently value yourself.

- **Determine the repair method:** The solution to a mental foundational crack is always one of two things: rediscovering who you are or finding YOUR genius (and sometimes both).

- **Address the root cause:** You can go through a situation so many times that you start thinking you *are* the situation. We can fail so many times that we start to think we *are* failures. Is the root of your problem failure or loss? Losing something or someone can make you feel lost, but you are not the loss.

- **Maintain the solution:** Consistent maintenance is the most overlooked part of any process. You have to remind yourself of who you are and renew your mind daily.

Chapter 12

Spiritual Education

I come from what most would consider a Christian family. My mother, father, aunts, uncles, and grandparents all identified as Christians. They may not have been in church every Sunday, but they believed in God and in Jesus as Lord and Savior.

I was baptized when I was twelve, and I vividly remember the experience. My paternal grandmother went to a traditional Baptist church—choir robes, deacons, and nurses in white gloves. Whenever I stayed with her on the weekends, I went to church.

Every service ended with an altar call. The pastor would say, "The doors of the church are open." In the early nineties, many sermons focused heavily on salvation, baptism, and avoiding hell. But on this particular Sunday, the message also spoke of Jesus as our hope and help. It was that hope and help I so badly needed.

I felt a pull. It was as if God Himself was calling me to that altar. My palms were sweaty and I was nervous, but I mustered the courage and went. I gave my life to the Lord.

I was baptized a few weeks later. My grandmother invited everyone. I remember the deacons singing "I wonder if the lighthouse will shine on me." It was a calming distraction from my nerves. When I came up from the water, I felt different. I felt free! It felt like a huge weight had been lifted off my twelve-year-old body. I had a strong sense that I was no longer alone.

When I say "spiritual education," I'm talking about anything that teaches you about your connection to the Source—anything that helps you understand the God in you.

The Bible

By far, the Bible has been the most beneficial resource for my spiritual education. I suggest you read it for yourself without a religious "lens." The Bible contains the greatest collection of true principles. Whether every story is historically literal or not, the principles endure. They apply to life today; they don't change or expire.

Church, Christianity, and Religion

Church can be a great introduction to God, but it is not enough. Why? Because religion without relationship can never be enough. Religion teaches you what was done by the "masters"; spiritual education teaches you how to *be* a master.

Recommended Resources for Spiritual Education:

- **Wayne Dyer:** Known as the "father of motivation." I highly recommend *The Power of Intention* and *Wishes Fulfilled.*

- **Myles Munroe:** He taught me the difference between religion and relationship. Read *Rediscovering the Kingdom.*

- **Neville Goddard:** One of the most influential spiritual thinkers of all time.

- **Reverend Ike:** He was flamboyant and bold about the message of "the God within you." His sermons on YouTube are gold.

Chapter 13

Discovering the Real YOU (I AM)

When building a new home, the first thing you do after drawing up plans is pour the foundation. It supports the weight of everything added to it. So, let me ask: How big is your life? Do you carry big responsibilities? Do you feel the weight of everything on you?

Knowing the real you is your foundation. "Who are you?" is the most uncomfortable question anyone can ask. When I first tried to answer this as an adult, I went straight to my roles: husband, father, Realtor. While these were facts, they were also all **EGO**.

Everything After Its Own Kind

When a dog has a child, it's a dog. When a cat has a child, it's a cat. Everything produces after its own kind. If many people consider themselves children of God, why don't we consider ourselves God?

Let me just rip the band-aid off: **You are God.** You are God in the Earth. Knowing the God in you is your firm foundation.

If this is your first time hearing this, it might sound blasphemous. But as I studied the Bible without a religious lens, it was right there:

> *"Let this mind be in you, which was also in Christ*
> *Jesus: Who being in the form of God, thought it*
> *not robbery to be equal with God"*
> Philippians 2:5-6 KJV

I am not saying I am God and you are not. I am saying Namaste: I honor the God in you, which also lives in me.
Think of God as the ocean. If you fill a bucket with water from
the ocean, that water is still the ocean. Religion says, "It's just
a bucket." The ego says, "It's just a cup." The Source says you
are the ocean in a body.

Knowing this is life-changing. I don't recommend walking
around shouting "I am God!" to everyone, but once you know
it, you don't have to defend it. Just be the love of God on Earth,
and people will see the God in you.

Chapter 14

Discovering YOUR Genius

Now that we have the foundation, we can build. Restoration focuses on the systems that make a house run: plumbing, electrical, HVAC. Without these, a house might look good but won't function.

For over a decade, I tried to fit into a puzzle where I didn't belong. I was an average Realtor because I hadn't discovered **My Genius**—my unique gift and purpose.

Your genius is the thing you do so well it borders on the supernatural. And yes, you have one. It might just be buried under the pressure of "being realistic."

How I Discovered My Genius

When the market crashed in 2009, I was forced to explore other ways to provide. At the time, I was teaching a Wednesday night Bible study. I loved creating illustrations that made scriptures relevant to everyday life. My pastor told me, "I see you doing stuff like this on YouTube." Every spiritual gift assessment I took said the same thing: knowledge and teaching.

Looking back, the clues were there since childhood:

- **Peer Mediation:** In 5th grade, I was a peer mediator. That was "life coaching" before life coaching was a thing!

- **Spelling Bees:** I won the school spelling bee. I had a natural interest in words and ideas.

- **Top Producer:** As a Realtor, I bought sales software, but the only part I used was the section containing quotes from successful entrepreneurs. I printed them out and made a book. I wasn't interested in the sales tools; I was interested in the wisdom.

Questions to Find Your Genius:

- **What do you think about most throughout the day?** (For me: Ideas and creative solutions.)

- **What comes easily to you but is extremely difficult for others?** Steve Harvey says your gift is what you do best with the least amount of effort.

- **What makes you angry?** (For me: Bad writing in movies.) Your gift is often tied to the things you notice that others miss.

- **What work doesn't feel like work?** What activities make you lose track of time?

- **What would you do for free?** What would you do even if there were no paycheck, just for the reward of doing it?

- **Are you an Architect, Builder, or Realtor?** Are you a visionary, a hands-on worker, or a salesperson? I tried to be a Realtor for 20 years, even though I was actually an architect.

Chapter 15

Rediscovering Your Passion

It's tough to do something day in and day out with excellence if you don't have passion. Dreams don't die; they just get buried under responsibilities.

You must believe that you can provide for your family **AND** do what you love. Let's go back to real estate: Survive on the structure (the mechanics), but thrive on the interior design (the joy). A life focused only on surviving is like a house with a furnace but no furniture.

It's time to update your life with things that make you happy. Decide that your life will be an **"AND"**:

- Responsible **AND** joyful

- Productive **AND** passionate

- Stable **AND** fulfilled

Rediscovering your passion doesn't make you irresponsible; it makes you better at everything else.

Chapter 16

Finding Your Purpose in Service

Your Genius will not grow on its own; you have to place demands on it. As Wayne Dyer wrote, "Your purpose will always be found in service." To serve is to give your gift to those who need it.

If you aren't sure how to start, here is a cheat code: start by helping someone else who is already using their gifts.

Look at Keith Lee, the food critic. He started doing reviews from a tiny chair to overcome social anxiety. His service saved dozens of businesses. He served others with a gift he didn't even know he had.

My journey started with service, too. I mentored young boys, wrote a motivational blog for friends, and coached my son's sports teams. I had been coaching and writing for a decade before I realized *that* was my genius, not selling houses.

Seeing something you created have a positive impact on someone else is the best confidence boost you can get. That is the God in you connecting with the God in others.

PHASE 4: IMPROVEMENT

Chapter 17

Meditation

In my journey, meditation has been one of the most beneficial additions to my life. I have been meditating for over 10 years, and it's now as vital to me as prayer, sleep, or eating. If I skip it, my whole day feels "off."

I compare meditation to installing air conditioning in a house that didn't have any; it changes the atmosphere instantly. It is a major stress reducer. While it doesn't stop stress from happening, it helps you manage it.

As we discussed in Chapter 8, the average person has thousands of thoughts a day—most of them negative. Meditation is the "dolly" of the mind; it helps you move the old junk out to make room for the new.

How to Meditate

Meditation is not a "demonic" or "tree-hugger" practice. It has existed for thousands of years. Just as everyone who prays isn't a Christian, everyone who meditates isn't a Buddhist.

"I Am" Meditation I developed this simple method to help people get started without needing a "guru":

- **Find a quiet place:** A bedroom or even a closet works. Eliminate the TV and radio.

- **Get comfortable:** Use a chair with a straight back. If you sit cross-legged and your legs "fall asleep," just use a chair.

- **Position your hands:** Place your palms on your thighs, either up or down.

- .**Focus on the breath:** Take a deep breath in and say "**I**" in your head. Take a deep breath out and say "**AM**."

Repeat this for fifteen minutes. When your mind drifts (and it will), simply return to the mantra: *I... AM...*

Chapter 18

Exercise and Appearance

Exercise is a must in Mind Rehab. Many people exercise to lose weight, but in this process, we exercise to get in mental shape. It is a massive stress reliever and confidence booster.

My Suggestions:

- **Consistency:** Aim for at least three times per week.

- **The Power of Walking:** Long walks work wonders for clarity. Your next big idea could be just one walk away.

- **The Sauna:** I call this "healing heat." Spending 15 minutes in a sauna helps flush out toxins, improves circulation, and relaxes the muscles. (Just remember to stay hydrated!)

Appearance: The External Flip

Simply put: when you look good, you feel good. It's time to level up your appearance and dress like the person you are becoming.

For years, I put myself on the back burner. I made sure my kids had nice clothes while I wore dress shoes until the heels were so worn down that I was literally digging rocks out of the soles with a pen. I thought I was being a "good father," but I was actually devaluing myself.

When I moved to Las Vegas in 2019, I had a "glow-up." I started investing in my shoe game—Jordans, Yeezys, and Tom Fords. I'm not telling you to spend beyond your means, but I am telling you to be your best self. If you rock braids, make them crispy. If you wear J's, keep them clean. Don't let your outward appearance distract people from seeing the real you.

74

Chapter 19

Diet and Intake

What goes in must come out. This isn't just about food; it's about what you consume via movies, music, and social media. If you watch horror movies all night, don't be surprised if you live in fear.

Your Nighttime Ritual

I have moved from "falling asleep" (being awake until I crash) to "going to sleep" (an intentional end to the night). Your subconscious doesn't have an off button. If you go to bed worried, your brain will run that "worry program" all night.

Nighttime Recommendations:

- **Affirmations:** Listen to or read things you want to manifest.

- **Gratitude:** Thank God for another day.

- **Visualization:** Picture your tomorrow going exactly the way you want it to.

Food and Wellness

Based on my experience, here are the dietary improvements that aid mental wellness:

- **Identify Intolerances:** Under stress, sensitivities to things like dairy or gluten are heightened. I discovered I was lactose intolerant at 13 and gluten-sensitive in my 30s. Cutting these out ended years of unexplained pain and bloating.

- **Alkaline Water:** Your brain is 75% water. Hydration impacts focus and mental clarity.

- **Green Vegetables:** Leafy greens help regulate the stress response.

- **Reduce High-Fat Foods:** Greasy, processed fats can interfere with serotonin—the "feel-good" chemical.

- **Limit Late-Night Drinking:** Alcohol harms the quality of your sleep. My wife and I have a "celebrate only" rule—we never drink because we had a bad day. Don't use alcohol as a crutch.

When you feel better, you think better. When you think better, you make better decisions.

Chapter 20:

Landscaping Your Environment for Success

One of the most important things to focus on when rehabbing a house is curb appeal. You can spend thousands of dollars and invest hundreds of hours into the interior, but if you skimp on the landscaping, it could all be for nothing. The outside should set the tone for the great work you've done on the inside. These next chapters anchor the spiritual and the practical transition of the book. Ready? Let's move on to Phase 4: Improvement and Phase 5: Maintaining.

Unfortunately, much of the world still judges a book by its cover. Landscaping your environment helps attract and push you toward what you **R.E.A.L.L.Y.** want. This means being mindful of the company you keep. Are you hanging out with people who share your new mindset, or are you stuck in environments that drain your energy? Remember: people treat you how YOU treat you. When you landscape an aura of success and respect around yourself, the world responds in kind.

Organize Your Environment, Organize Your Life

Most improvements come from having the discipline to do the simple things consistently.

- **Organize your workspace:** When my desk is a mess, my thoughts are a mess. Organizing your workspace allows your mind to function with more clarity.

- **Clean your closet:** You go into your closet every day. If it takes you forever to find what to wear, you are wasting decision-making energy. Billionaires like Mark Zuckerberg wear the same thing daily to save that mental energy for bigger tasks. Faster decisions lead to faster visible change.

- **Keep your car clean:** I once had a pastor tell me, "I can tell everything about a man by the way he keeps his trunk." It sounds like a reach, but it's true. As you tidy up the spaces you inhabit—like your center console or your trunk—you tidy up your life.

- **Make your bed:** A made-up bed has a positive psychological effect. It shows respect for the place where you spend the most time. That small "win" first thing in the morning provides an emotional boost that carries through the day.

Window Shop

Visualizing is the first step toward manifesting. Cruise past the dealership of your dream car. Go to an open house for a property you "on paper" have no business looking at. You must have it in your head and heart before you can have it in your hand.

Chapter 21

The Calculated Risk Formula

A risk is the possibility of losing something of value, but the riskiest thing you can do is take no risks at all. The key is to take **calculated** risks.

When I bought my first property at 22—a two-family building with a condemned bar—I miscalculated the time and money it would take. A four-month project turned into ten months. But the risk was worth it because it taught me the process.

The Calculated Risk Formula:

Proper Knowledge + Realistic Timeline + Counting the Cost = A Calculated Risk

- **Proper Knowledge:** Never invest in a business (or a relationship) you don't understand.

- **Realistic Timeline:** Time is a limited commodity. Be honest about how long it will take to see a return.

- **Counting the Cost:** Determine the financial and emotional sacrifices required before you see gains.

Chapter 22

Improvements Based on the Real YOU

Once you know the God in You and your Genius, you can make major changes with confidence. You no longer settle for relationships or organizations that control you because you know what you deserve.

I spent ten years trying to be a top-producing Realtor because I wanted to be like my successful uncle. But I never asked if I had the gifts for it. I was a "slow learner," mistaking "my smart" for "my Genius."

In real estate, we have a term: **Highest and Best Use**. It's the use that makes a property most valuable. You must find the highest and best use for your life. Is it more valuable for me to rehab a house for a profit, or to help a thousand people rehab their minds? When you find your highest and best use, even your past mistakes start to work for your good.

PHASE 5: MAINTAINING

Chapter 23

Scheduled Maintenance of Your Rehabbed Mind

Maintaining a home requires keeping the grass cut and changing the furnace filters. Your mindset is no different. You must choose each day to be host of to God rather than a hostage to your ego.

Many people fall off in the maintenance phase. The best way to describe this phase is as a *practice*. Doctors and lawyers have a "practice"—it doesn't mean they don't know what they're doing; it means they are continually working on the quality of their craft.

Attend Workshops and Seek Coaching

I spent $30,000 on a year of investment coaching. It didn't magically make me a millionaire overnight, but it gave me the systems and the confidence to scale. People value what they pay for. Invest in yourself.

My Experience with Therapy

Before I moved to Las Vegas, I hit rock bottom. I thought my only options were to win the lottery or end my life. I sought therapy and discovered why they call therapists "shrinks"—they help you *shrink* a problem that feels unmanageable down to a size you can handle. Never make a permanent decision for a temporary situation.

Chapter 24

The Power of Community

The journey to higher awareness can be lonely, but there is power in having a huddle. Relationship means honoring the God in someone else. My wife and I are opposites; my Genius is her weakness and vice versa. Together, we make magic.

Monday Night Huddle

I started a men's group that combines Monday Night Football with real talk about personal development. Seeing men heal and prioritize themselves is the most fulfilling work I've ever done.

Get into a community with people who are on the same path. It makes the world go round.

Chapter 25

The Eight-Billion-Piece Puzzle

I view the world as an eight-billion-piece puzzle. Billions of pieces are currently out of place, trying to fit into spaces where they don't belong. This hurts the person and the people around them.

Every time you discover your purpose and fill the space God designed you for, the world looks a little better. You can literally change the world by simply being your true self and doing what you love.

Finish your breakfast, Rehabber. The world is waiting for your piece of the puzzle.

Appendix

Scripture References

- *Where there is no vision, the people perish.* Proverbs 29:18 KJV

- *For God does not show favoritism.* Romans 2:11 NIV

- *"The Kingdom of God is within."* Luke 17:21 NIV

- *Do not conform to the pattern of this world, but be transformed by the renewing of your mind.* Romans 12:2 NIV

- *For I am convinced that neither death nor life, neither angels nor demons, neither the present nor future, nor any powers, neither height nor depth, nor anything else in all creation, will be able to separate us from the love of God...* Romans 8:38-39 NIV

- *Let this mind be in you, which was also in Christ Jesus: <u>Who being in the form of God,</u> thought it not robbery <u>to be equal with God.</u>* Philippians 2:5-6 KJV (emphasis added)

- *Your attitude should be the same as that of Christ Jesus.* Philippians 2:5 NLT

- *"Let us make man in our image, in our likeness..."* Genesis 1:26 NIV

- *So God created man in his own image, in the image of God he created him; male and female he created them.* Genesis 1:27 NIV

- *"I and the Father are one."* John 10:30 NIV

- *"We are not stoning you for any of these"' replied the Jew. "But for blasphemy, because you, a mere man, claim to be God."' Jesus answered them, "Is it not written in your law, I have said you are gods?"* (John 10:33-34) NIV

- *"I have said you are gods, you are sons of the Most High. But you will die like mere men, you will fall like every other ruler."* Psalms 82:6-7 NIV

- *"According to your faith…"* (Matthew 9:29) NIV

- *"A student is not above his teacher, nor a servant above his master. <u>It is enough for the student to be like his teacher and the servant like his master.</u>* Matthew 10:24-25 NIV (emphasis added)

- *"He who receives you receives me, and <u>he who receives me receives the one who sent me</u>."* Matthew 10:40 NLT (emphasis added)

- *"He will reply, 'I tell you the truth, whatever you did not do for one of <u>the least of these,</u> you did not do for me."* Matthew 25:45 NIV (emphasis added)

- *"For where two or three come together in my name, there am I with them."* Matthew 18:20 NIV

- *"The most important one," answered Jesus, "is this: Hear O Israel, the Lord our God, <u>the Lord is one.</u> Love the Lord you*

God with all your heart and with all your soul and with all your mind and with all your strength. The second is this: Love your neighbor as yourself. There is no commandment greater than these." Mark 12:29-30 NIV (emphasis added)

- *"My mother and brothers are those who hear God's word and <u>put it into practice</u>."* Luke 8:21NIV(emphasis added)

- *Holy Father, protect them <u>by the power of your name</u>—the name you gave me—<u>so that they may be one as we are one.</u>* John 17:11 NIV(emphasis added)

- *For God does not show favoritism.* Romans 2:11 NIV

- *Whatever you do, work at it with all your heart, <u>as working for the Lord</u>, not for men.* Colossians 3:23 NIV (emphasis added)

- <u>*Both the one who makes men holy and those who are made holy are of the same family,*</u> *so Jesus is not ashamed to call them brothers.* Hebrews 2:11 NIV (emphasis added)

- *"This is how we know <u>we are in him</u>; Whoever claims to live in him must walk as Jesus did."* 1 John 2:5 NIV

- *God is love, whoever lives in love lives in God, and God in him.* 1 John 4:16 NIV

- *"The kingdom of God does not come with your careful observation, nor will people say, 'Here it is',or 'There it is', because the kingdom of God is within you."* Luke 17:20-21 NIV

- *Do not conform to the pattern of this world, but be transformed by the renewing of your mind.* Romans 12:2 NIV

- *They devoted themselves to the apostles' teaching and to fellowship, to the breaking of bread and to prayer. Everyone was filled with awe at the many wonders and signs performed by the apostles. All the believers were together and had everything in common. They sold property and possessions to give to anyone who had need. Every day they continued to meet together in the temple courts. They broke bread in their homes and ate together with glad and sincere hearts, praising God and enjoying the favor of all the people. Acts 2:42-47 NIV*

Works Cited

Arnault, Bernard. "Bernard Arnault." *Wikipedia*, Wikimedia Foundation, en.wikipedia.org/wiki/Bernard_Arnault. Accessed 19 Mar. 2026.

Dyer, Wayne W. *The Power of Intention: Learning to Co-create Your World Your Way.* Hay House, 2004.

---. *Wishes Fulfilled: Mastering the Art of Manifesting.* Hay House, 2012.

Eikerenkoetter, Frederick. Rev. Ike's Secrets For Health, Joy and Prosperity, For YOU: A Science Of Living Study Guide. Science of Living Publications.

Gallup. "CliftonStrengths Assessment." *Gallup*, www.gallup.com/cliftonstrengths/en/252137/home.aspx. Accessed 19 Mar. 2026.

Gaston, Deborah A. *Finding Your F.L.O.W.: Answering the Writer's Call through Faith, Love, Obedience and Worship.* 2018.

Goddard, Neville. *The Neville Goddard Deluxe Collection.* Edited by Noah Press, 2017.

Hansen, Mark Victor, and Xavier Eikerenkoetter. *Reverend Ike: An Extraordinary Life of Influence*. 2021

Harvey, Steve. "Success Habits." *YouTube*, 3x3rEg2qvcQ. Accessed 19 Mar. 2026.

Hendricks, Gay. *The Big Leap: Conquer Your Hidden Fear and Take Life to the Next Level*. HarperOne, 2009.

Jay-Z. "Public Service Announcement (Interlude)." *The Black Album*, Roc-A-Fella/Def Jam, 2003.

Maharishi Foundation USA. *Transcendental Meditation (TM)*, Tm.org. Accessed 19 Mar. 2026.

McQuarrie, Christopher, screenwriter. *The Usual Suspects*. Directed by Bryan Singer, PolyGram Visual Programming, 1995.

Munroe, Myles. *Rediscovering the Kingdom: Ancient Hope for Our 21st Century World*. Destiny Image Publishers, 2004.

"Rev. Ike." *The Week*, 8 Jan. 2015, theweek.com/articles/503026/rev-ike.

Rev. Ike Legacy. YouTube, www.youtube.com/@RevIkeLegacy. Accessed 19 Mar. 2026.

"Shine on Me." *Traditional African American Spiritual*, Public Domain.

Yoshida, Tadao. "Tadao Yoshida." *Wikipedia*, Wikimedia Foundation, en.wikipedia.org/wiki/YKK. Accessed 19 Mar. 2026.

About the Author

Jameen R. Willis is a visionary and creative force in personal development and business ideation. His ability to simplify complex ideas and turn them into practical systems has made him a highly sought-after author, coach, and consultant.

Inspired by spending over 25 years in real estate sales, investing, and property management, he developed the Mind Rehab Process — a renovation blueprint for the mind inspired by the principles of rehabbing and restoring property.

Through his coaching, consulting, and writing, he equips individuals with practical frameworks to strengthen their thinking, rebuild from the inside out, and move forward with clarity, confidence, and purpose.